He Who Calls is Faithful

VICKI ALICIA

WESTBOW·
PRESS
A DIVISION OF THOMAS NELSON
& ZONDERVAN

Scripture taken from The Living Bible copyright © 1971 by Tyndale House
Foundation. Used by permission of Tyndale House Publishers Inc., Carol
Stream, Illinois 60188. All rights reserved. The Living Bible, TLB, and the The
Living Bible logo are registered trademarks of Tyndale House Publishers.

WestBow Press books may be ordered through booksellers or by contacting:

WestBow Press
A Division of Thomas Nelson & Zondervan
1663 Liberty Drive
Bloomington, IN 47403
www.westbowpress.com
1 (866) 928-1240

ISBN: 978-1-4908-5349-9 (sc)
ISBN: 978-1-4908-5348-2 (e)

Library of Congress Control Number: 2014917334

Printed in the United States of America.

WestBow Press rev. date: 10/3/2014

Dedicated to

My children, Julie and Wayne,
who travelled with me on this
pathway of change.

Their faithfulness, love, and courage
in the midst of confusion and suffering
have been and continue to be
a great inspiration in my life.

"All your children shall be taught
of the Lord, and great shall be
the peace of your children." (Isaiah 54:13)

Contents

Foreword...ix

Preface xi

Acknowledgments...xiii

Introduction..xv

Faith Is Having Confidence in the Testimony of Another 1

The Heart of God 3

No Place for a Fragile Heart...5

My Not-So-Grand Entrance 7

Winds of Adversity and Occasional Rays of Sunshine 9

In Whom Do We Trust?..11

A Ray of Hope in the Midst of the Storm...........................13

All That Glitters Is not Necessarily Gold 15

A Light Shines in the Darkness 17

Today 23

The First Step 27

God's Love...30

The Way 33

God's Beauty 36

A Loving Spark..40

Castles in the Sand...43

A Child's Plea 46

Memories...50

Sharing with Friends 53

Peace 56

Take a Step 59

Tears of Love 62

Praise God 65

To Walk with God's Spirit 69

Epilogue 73

About the Author 75

Foreword

I remember in our very early days of knowing Vicki Alicia, we were outside the manse gate in Kalgoorlie. I was there to say goodbye and was about to put my arm around her and give her a hug. I suddenly realised this beautiful young mother was not ready for hugs. She had a high emotional wall around her and was not ready to let me in just yet.

I can hardly believe that was thirty-five years ago. Vicki has been a part of our family for that long. She has walked with us through joys and sorrows, tears and laughter, even our deepest tragedies.

It did not take long for me to see that even though Vicki was inward looking and cautious, she was a wonderful mother to her two children. She was also very creative, an artist, a poet, and always longing to write her experiences.

One day I knew the walls around her heart had come down. She suddenly became ready for affection, for kindness to be received and given, and for her infectious laughter to be heard.

This book is part of that. So much to share of the healing work of the Lord. Healing and restoration within and being lived out in daily life. I expect all who read this book will both enjoy and be encouraged page by page.

Thank you, Vicki, for sharing your heart with us.

Isabel Paterson
Pastor, author, nurse, missionary

Preface

The God who commanded the light to shine out of darkness is the same God who shines the glorious light of Jesus in our hearts. He is faithful, and His Word has become a lamp unto my feet and a light unto my path.

My heart had been hardened by many, many years of pain, suffering, and circumstances beyond my control. Determination that I would never allow anyone to get close enough to hurt me again isolated a heart that was lonely and desperate for love.

My journey towards faith, hope, and love began with a simple prayer in the middle of the night: "If there is a God, please help me." He had been waiting for me to ask for His help and immediately set in motion a way of escape.

Encouraged by the example of other Christians and new understanding of the faithfulness and promises of God, I took tiny steps of faith. It was as though each new stepping stone across a river of confusion brought challenges and joy. I understood that although my feet often got wet as I stumbled, Jesus was walking beside me and would not allow me to fall.

At the end of each new experience, the Lord gave me the ability to record in poems the preciousness of each step. Prior to writing these verses, I had not ever written any poetry, and there is just no way in the natural I could have done so.

I have always felt that I may be called on one day to publish the poems and believe the time to do so is now. My hope and prayer is that they will bless and encourage you and lead you to earnestly seek a closer relationship with the living God.

Acknowledgments

I wish to acknowledge the help of my family and friends in the writing of this part of my earlier life. For the love, encouragement, and support they provided and which has given me the courage and confidence needed to do this.

In particular, I thank Isabel Paterson, whose late husband, Trevor, was my first and dearest pastor. They embraced me with love and gave me hope.

He lifted me out of the pit of despair, out from the bog and the mire, and set my feet on a hard, firm path, and steadied me as I walked along. He has given me a new song to sing, of praises to our God. Now many will hear of the glorious things he did for me, and stand in awe before the Lord, and put their trust in him. (Psalm 40:2–3)

Introduction

He Who Calls Is Faithful

The title of this book is based on the promises and faithfulness of a gracious and loving God, who calls us out of bondage and brokenness into a glorious covenant relationship with Him.

For all who may be broken-hearted, battered, and bruised by a life of confusion, misunderstanding, and fear, take courage, because God is a loving, heavenly Father. He knows us intimately and loves us with an unfathomable love. When we acknowledge who He is and step out in faith, He leads us into a wonderfully personal relationship full of joy, peace, and promise.

The call of God is not only to those who need His healing touch in their lives but unto all who have been blessed with stability, love, and peace in their family relationships, so they may help others less fortunate. This book will encourage any who truly desire to comfort the lonely and broken-hearted, and to lead them to a place of peace and security. The author reveals personal details of her grief and suffering as a means of identifying with and encouraging the reader.

Fear not; for you will no longer live in shame. The shame of your youth and the sorrows of your widowhood will be remembered no more. For your creator will be your "husband". The Lord of Hosts is his name; He is your Redeemer, the Holy One of Israel, the God of all the earth. For the Lord has called you back from your grief. (Isaiah 54:4–6).

Prayer

Father God, you heard my cry of desperation and answered with love, mercy, and grace, lifting me from the depths of fear, confusion, and frustration to a place where I can enjoy comfort, peace, eternal security, and joy. May all who have the opportunity to read my life story be inspired and encouraged to trust You with their lives so that You, Lord, may pour out Your love and blessings upon them. Amen.

Faith Is Having Confidence in the Testimony of Another

Words are powerful and have the ability to build people up or tear them down. From an early age, we are taught by our parents or primary caregivers. If their examples are loving and honest, we learn to trust in what we hear and have no problem acting on their words of wisdom. However, if for any reason they are not able to provide a safe, loving environment, our development, ability to trust, self-esteem, and social skills will be seriously affected. We realize our survival is totally dependent on our own ability to meet our basic needs. We will trust only what we can see and control.

If we have not been able to trust in authority figures we can see, how can we be expected to trust in a God we cannot see? When words spoken to us in our formative years caused doubt and confusion, being told to simply trust God's Word does not work.

Words have the power and authority to influence lives and bring about tremendous change. But unless we believe in the sincerity of their authors, it is like water off a duck's back.

For real change to take effect, the broken-hearted need to hear words of encouragement and promise supported by loving examples.

We cannot begin a journey of faith without first hearing God's Word, because it reveals not only His promises, provisions, and protection but also His character.

What is faith?

It is the confident assurance that something we want is going to happen. It is the certainty that what we hope for is waiting for us, even if we cannot see it up ahead. You can never please God without faith, without depending on him, anyone who wants to come to God must believe that there is a God and that he rewards those who sincerely look for him. (Hebrews 11:1, 6)

It is one thing to know of God and yet another entirely to know Him and His personality, character, and heart's desire for each and every one of us.

The Heart of God

The Lord cares for you,
the Lord loves you, and the Lord desires you.

He desires your praise,
and He desires your presence.
He longs to hear you worship Him.
He loves to hear the songs of rejoicing.
He longs to hear the heart of praise.
He longs to hear you say that you love Him.

Yes, the Lord Himself cared for you
when no one had time for you.
He has time, and He loves you so much.
He has so much planned for you.

Oh, if only your heart could grasp
those things that He has for you.
If only your heart would desire more,
for as you desire more, you will receive more of Him.

*Oh, if only you could see all those things
that He has planned and desired
and purposed so far in your life.*

*But He would also love you to see
that He has much planned for you in the future,
for He has saved you for a purpose.
He has redeemed your life from destruction,
and He has crowned your head with loving kindness.*

I received these words of encouragement from the Lord many years ago. They have been and continue to be a tremendous inspiration in my daily walk with Him.

No Place for a Fragile Heart

I was born and raised in Boulder, the twin city, gold-mining town of Kalgoorlie in Western Australia, approximately 600 kilometres (350 miles) east of Perth, the state capital. The climate there is extremely harsh, with summer temperatures in the high-forty degrees Celsius (over one hundred degrees Fahrenheit). Occasionally, we would get mild relief from the endless days and nights of unbearable heat (and annoying flies) in the form of a late-afternoon breeze known as the "Esperance Doctor." This is a wind that comes up from the Southern Ocean, 350 miles away, where the coastal town of Esperance is situated.

Rain is scarce, but when it does come, it is accompanied by deafening thunder and lightning that illuminates the whole sky. The red earth, hardened by extreme heat and dry easterly winds, is unable to contain the torrential rain that floods the plains, turning the ground into a muddy red quagmire.

Winter in Kalgoorlie is bitterly cold, with overnight temperatures plummeting to zero and causing the water to freeze in pipes. By midday, provided shelter from the wind can be found, the sun manages to warm everything, and the days can be very pleasant.

During my childhood, most housing in Kalgoorlie was made of weatherboard and tin sheeting, with no insulation and no air conditioning. As a result, the temperature inside our house became unbearable during summer. The only way you could gain relief from it was to sleep outside in the open, where it was marginally cooler. This presented its own problems due to the invasion of insects, particularly mosquitoes. Mosquito nets were not available, so we used to hide under our sheets instead, which just made us even hotter. During winter, the only heating we had was a solitary paraffin heater we would all huddle around.

Being a typical mining town, Kalgoorlie had a hotel located on every main street corner, and most of the men spent their free time drinking with their workmates and friends. Springtime, with its mild conditions, was an ideal time for the famous, local, annual racing carnival, the highlight of the year. A man could make his fortune, or lose all his savings, by betting on the horses. The compulsion to gamble was very strong in Kalgoorlie.

The intense, unpredictable outback storms characterized the emotional turmoil in my life and relationships. As a result, I built layer upon layer of protective emotional walls around my fragile heart.

My Not-So-Grand Entrance

My entry into the world was premature by two months. Being so small and fragile, I needed to be wrapped in cotton wool for warmth and remained in hospital at least six weeks after my mother was discharged. Because my family lived some distance from the hospital and with limited public transport, it was virtually impossible for my mother and siblings to visit.

Fortunately, my uncle owned a motorcycle and offered to deliver my mother's expressed milk to the hospital. He did this faithfully for three weeks, or until he heard one of the nurses commenting, "Here comes the milkman!" This upset him so much he abruptly stopped delivering.

The nursing staff did everything they could to meet my physical needs. However, there is no substitute for the relationship and bonding that takes place between a newborn infant and his or her mother. My emotional need for love and comfort could not be met, and this lacking would later lead to a sense of abandonment.

My father had chosen a name well before I was born, but my mother had other ideas. She had set her heart on the name Vicki Alicia if I was a girl. It was a miracle that she managed to persuade my father to change his mind, because he always got his own way. Though my parents did not know it at the time, the name I was given would later influence my character and my destiny.

Vicki means "victorious spirit," and Alicia means "truth." Together they imply a defender of the less fortunate and an upholder of the rights of others.

Fine threads of gold in the form of faith, hope, and love were woven into the tapestry of my life and would ensure my survival. Red dust storms and muddy waters often flooded my soul and tried to disguise these God-given treasures, but He had placed in me a desire to uncover the beauty of these golden threads that lay dormant for many years. This was to become my motivation in life and the main reason I was able to eventually overcome seemingly insurmountable obstacles on the pathway of my life.

> You made all the delicate, inner parts of my body, and knit them together in my mother's womb. Thank you for making me so wonderfully complex! It is amazing to think about. Your workmanship is marvellous and how well I know it. You were there while I was being formed in utter seclusion! You saw me before I was born and scheduled each day of my life before I began to breathe. (Psalm 139:13–16)

Winds of Adversity and Occasional Rays of Sunshine

When I had reached my goal weight in hospital and was allowed to go home to my mother, I was smothered in love and affection by my brother and sister, making up for what I had sorely missed during my first four weeks of life in hospital. At the time, my elder sister was three years old. Even at that tender age, she displayed abundant love and compassion. My two-year-old brother had a gentle nature and peaceful spirit. They would later combine to become a tower of strength and a place of refuge when the turbulent times came that would plague our lives.

My mother had given birth to eight children by the age of twenty-six. Two of them died within a few days of being born, and their birthdays were always marked on the calendar as special days to remember. I know now that being exposed to the reality of death and grief at such a young age touched my heart deeply and had a marked effect on the rest of my life.

The responsibility of having to care for six young children, and at the same time deal with a demanding husband was very difficult for my mother. My father was like a child himself in many ways, always wanting attention, determined to win at all costs, and bullying anyone who stood in his way.

It became apparent as I got older that I was born with a strong sense of right and wrong. At some point in my childhood, I made a conscious decision to become the defender of my family and purposed in my heart to stand up to my father's unreasonable demands. Many David and Goliath battles would be fought which were, of course, impossible to win. But that did not stop me from trying.

The obvious resentment I felt towards him, and the defiant look I gave when challenged, roared silently within me, "You may have my obedience and loyalty when it is enforced, but you will never have my love or my respect." And my father could tell. Unfortunately, survival skills of rebellion and rejection would also take root in my heart and create distrust with male authority figures.

As children, during daylight hours we spent as much time as possible away from our home. In those days, Kalgoorlie-Boulder was a great place to play, and we were blessed with the freedom to roam around the town and nearby bush with our friends. We spent many hours exploring abandoned mining buildings, hunting for perceived "treasures" in the bush, and sometimes getting into mischief.

In Whom Do We Trust?

The most important relationships formed as a child growing up in a mining town were with my brothers and sisters. We formed a special bond, no doubt from our challenging childhood circumstances.

Nevertheless there were good times, too, times when the bright Australian sunshine warmed the depth of our hearts. These included the times we spent with my grandmother, who lived not far from us in the same town. It was always a special occasion when we were able to visit her. I was happy there and felt safe and loved. My nana and pop had the most amazing back garden, filled with nooks and crannies, where we used to play and hunt for treasure.

My grandparents kept birds, and they had literally hundreds of little finches, budgerigars, and canaries. We used to spend hours watching them fly nonstop around the inside large cages. I was always fascinated by their ease, their sense purpose, and the amazing way they could quickly change direction.

There was also the large yellow and white cockatoo that sat in a cage near the back door. It used to dance and "talk," repeating phrases it had learned. Locally known as "cockies," these birds have been known to live for over a hundred years.

Pop collected scrap metal, and every corner of the yard was stockpiled with interesting objects. We played hide-and-seek there and loved the fruit from the trees in the back garden, which were allowed to eat when in season.

Pop had a sweet tooth. He loved his cup of tea and a slice of cake so much that after eating his portion of cake, he would suddenly thump the kitchen table with his clenched fist and shout, "Cake, Sarah! More cake!" He would then very generously share it with the rest of us.

I never knew whether my grandmother's rapid response to his outburst was out of love or fear, but whichever it was, I always remember her as the most loving, gentle, Christian lady you could possibly meet. My older sister formed a special bond with her and made a very determined effort to copy everything she did and to be like her.

Directly across the road from our childhood home lived my other grandmother, who was totally different. She was very strict and showed little love towards us, focusing more on loyalty and obedience. She displayed very little affection for us. This proved very difficult for a child who just wanted to be loved and comforted. The truth was that no one could live up to her unrealistic expectations, except my father, of course.

A Ray of Hope in the Midst of the Storm

I developed an intense stammering at a very early age, and it was difficult for me to pronounce certain letters of the alphabet. Being teased at school hampered my ability to express my thoughts and feelings.

During my second year at school, a teacher decided it would be good "therapy" for me to overcome my stammering by reading out loud in front of the class. My greatest fear was now a reality. Every student stopped what they were doing and focused on me slowly rising to my feet. I was unable to complete even one sentence without stammering and when finally excused, sat down. The intense shame from that incident stayed with me for many years and deepened my sense of loneliness and isolation.

Despite this and my tendency to withdraw, my teachers were very kind and did their best to try to help me overcome my feelings of inferiority and low self-esteem. In spite of my stammer, and due to the sympathy and considerate attitude from most of my teachers, I actually ended up doing well at school.

Mum did her utmost to provide for us at home. As often as she could afford to, she spoiled us with little parties on our birthdays. At Christmas-time, she always made sure we received lots of little presents. When we had to walk home from school in the middle of winter, in howling wind and drenching rain, hot soup and scones would be waiting for us.

My father always had money for drinking with his mates or betting on the racehorses, but he did not consider our education to be important. He refused to pay the small fee for me to sit my high school certificate, and I was forced into leaving school six weeks before the exam. I applied for a job at a local supermarket where my older sister worked. My ambition had always been to become a nurse, and I was totally devastated when it seemed impossible. However, even in those early days, I knew my destiny was not in my father's hands.

Despite my disappointment, I was determined to become a nurse, so I worked and saved to buy the required textbooks. By the grace of God, I was accepted for nursing training without the usual formal educational certificates.

Because I was only sixteen, I needed my father's consent. The thought of asking his permission was daunting, because I knew he would be against the idea. I knew I had to be very strong and resolute when I approached him. After a heated argument, during which he must have seen how determined I was, he finally consented but only on condition that I continued to live at home.

I loved nursing and studied day and night to achieve high marks. In doing so, I gained respect from my peers. Nursing is more a vocation than just a job and can be very trying, especially for a very young person. There are many challenges and difficult circumstances to cope with which you do not encounter in other fields. Unless your heart is truly in it, you will probably not survive the training.

I believe my inner strength and determined character, conditioned by years of adversity, helped me to deal with the stressful situations I found myself in training and as a nurse. It enabled me to be compassionate when dealing with hospital patients and their families. My dream of becoming a nurse having come true, my self-image improved, and I had a real sense of belonging.

All That Glitters Is not Necessarily Gold

As my career in nursing progressed, I started to feel much happier and confident. Yet I knew there was still something lacking in my life. I was aware of a deep desire to be loved and accepted in a personal way.

I met and fell in love with a local man my parents knew and seemed to approve of, and we married not long after I qualified as a nurse. Although I was only seventeen years of age, it was quite common in those days for girls to get married very young. I entered the marriage full of enthusiasm and hope, and for the first time in my life was truly happy. So happy in fact that I thought I had found the pot of gold at the end of the rainbow.

The sad truth is neither my husband nor myself were really prepared for the responsibility of marriage. I continued to work as a nurse, but constant financial instability created a situation whereby we lived in ten houses in the space of five years. Having to cope with a devastating miscarriage, loss of all our possessions in a house fire, and then the sudden and unexpected death of our son only two days after his birth dealt the final blow.

Our daughter was only three years old when we lost our infant son. Apart from my own pain from losing a precious newborn, I knew my daughter, even at that young age, was conscious of the loss.

Our son died in the ambulance being transferred from the hospital to the local airport, where he was to be flown by the Royal Flying Doctor Service to the city. I was not allowed to accompany him on this flight, and was informed several hours later that he had been flown directly to Perth for a cause of death to be determined.

As a nurse I understood the process that was taking place. But I grieved over the fact I had not been able to hold my infant son in my arms or say goodbye. It was also believed in those days that it was better for the mother not to be included in making the funeral arrangements and so on. All my son's baby clothes, pram, and new toys had been removed from the house without my knowledge. The only sense of reality for me was standing over a small white coffin at the graveside. It was as though my infant son had vanished off the face of the earth.

The depth of grief, loss, and confusion set me on a downward spiral of depression that caused me to come close to taking my own life on several occasions. Professional counselling was not recommended. One was expected to just get over it and move on with his or her life. My whole life had come crashing down around me, and my precious daughter became my total focus in life. I did not know then that some fifteen months later, I would be blessed with the safe arrival of another son.

The strain of trying to hold our marriage together eventually took its toll, and we separated. I was left with no home, no money, very little furniture, and two small children to raise and to try and provide some stability in their lives.

My family did their best to try and support me in this difficult situation, but no one could have foreseen the relational storm clouds gathering on the horizon. They would bring what seemed then to be insurmountable waves of fear and confusion that lasted four years.

Eventually, the children and I found somewhere to live and we settled into our new home.

A Light Shines in the Darkness

I was acutely aware that despite my best efforts, I had failed to provide my children with the emotional stability they needed and had been lacking in my own childhood. As hard as I might try, no amount of reasoning or justification could lift the burden of despair and hopelessness I carried. There just seemed to be no way out of my predicament. One night when my children were asleep, I remember crying out from the depth of my heart, "If there is a God, *please* help me!" Although I did not experience any immediate relief, I now know that God had begun to move in my life and hopeless circumstance.

Two weeks later, while driving to the shops, I saw a woman standing at a bus stop near my home. I recognised Desma, a woman I had not seen for over six months. We had met at a local women's support group meeting. She was a few years older than I and had two children. Desma was always withdrawn at the meetings and seemed to find it difficult to join in the various activities. Like all of us who attended these meetings, there were obviously issues in her life. I did not know what they were, but I liked her and felt drawn to her.

I decided to stop my car and offer her a lift into town, which she accepted. We had not gone very far when I became aware she was not the same Desma I spent time with six months previously. There was a dramatic change in her personality. Whereas she had previously appeared emotionally drained and lifeless, she now bubbled with enthusiasm and was full of joy. She was like a glass of freshly poured champagne, sparkling and overflowing. The contrast was truly amazing.

I asked her what had happened. She responded immediately, "I found Jesus!" I was so taken aback I found my hands gripping the steering wheel so tightly and wondered if I would ever be able to let go. At the same time, a fear rose inside me I did not really understand. My initial response was to stop the car and ask Desma to get out. But my conscience wouldn't let me. I knew it would only take a few more minutes to get to where I was to drop her off, so I let her continue to explain how her newfound faith in Jesus changed her life.

She invited me to go to church with her, and that really shook me. There was no way I could see myself going anywhere near a church. I declined as politely as I could and could not wait for her to get out of the car.

The strange thing is that as I drove away, I was overcome by a sense of relief and a feeling that, for some reason, I was back in control of my life. This was such an odd sensation. It felt as though I reached into a beehive, tasted pure sweet honey, and then immediately panicked and withdrew my hand.

When I attended Sunday school a couple times as a child, I saw pictures of Jesus holding a lamb. He looked gentle enough, but the fact He was God's Son was enough to scare me. I knew God had all power and authority, and as I believed I was unworthy, thought it best to avoid getting in His bad books.

One evening when I was about ten years old, a small group of friends thought it would be fun to go into the local church and steal some candles from the altar. We didn't need them or even really want them. We were just being mischievous.

The large wooden door creaked as it opened, and in single file, we crept down the moonlit aisle. The wooden ceiling creaked and groaned as we did so. Suddenly, a strong gust of wind slammed the heavy wooden door shut, and we bolted outside into the darkness, so sure it was God, and He was after us. I retained this fear of God and shied away from having anything to with Him or the church.

To me, Christians were "strange" and out to "get you." Even as a child, I crossed to the other side of the street to avoid the Salvation

Army workers on the street corner. I am sure other people in my life had tried to talk to me about God, but my pain and fear was always greater than my need. Somehow, my asking God for help opened the door of my heart to receive His love and grace.

Over the next three days I thought of Desma constantly and wrestled with what happened, wondering why our chance encounter affected me so deeply. I knew I wanted what Desma had, yet the whole idea filled me with fear. I was worried that I might be reaching too far outside my comfort level and would again lose control of my life. My deep-seated mistrust towards others made it very difficult for me to make decisions about my future. I was reluctant to do anything that might destroy what little hope I had left.

Not long after my encounter with Desma, I woke up one morning with a strong desire to bake. This was very odd, because anyone who knows me well will testify my interest in the kitchen is limited to "survival" cooking. But I had to bake something. I dropped my children off at school and went shopping at the local supermarket. By eleven o'clock that morning, I had baked several quiches, sausage rolls, and small apple pies. Baking had been a good distraction, but I still had three hours to fill before school finished.

In the stillness, thoughts of Desma and all the things she told me about Jesus and how her newfound friendship and trust in His faithfulness had changed her life so dramatically went through my mind. I decided there and then I would visit her, despite the apprehension I felt.

Delighted to see me and over several cups of coffee, Desma shared again how she experienced hope, love, and joy as she took small steps of faith. It seemed nothing could dampen her enthusiasm, joy, and boldness.

She asked me if she could take me to meet her pastor. I immediately baulked at the thought, but rather than rejecting her offer outright, I asked her for his address, saying I would go and see him later, by myself. I did this deliberately, as I was afraid of what I might be letting myself in for.

Time seemed to stand still that day. I baked, cleaned, visited Desma, and returned home. Still restless, and confused as to why I had felt compelled to bake that morning, I decided to drive to the pastor's house. The pathway leading from the gate to the front door of the manse seemed to go on forever. For every step I took forward, I wanted to take three steps back. I was met at the door by a lovely, soft-spoken, grey-haired man. I don't remember what I said to him, because, to be honest, I didn't really understand why I was there in the first place. After chatting for a short time, Pastor Trevor invited me to come and meet a young couple from the church.

As it turned out, they were holding a birthday party for one of the pastor's children. After being introduced to them, this lovely young couple invited myself and children to the party after school. I was keen to accept but I could not attend without a present or contributing in some fashion. A feeling of illegitimate shame and inadequacy immediately surfaced, and my brain scanned every recess to come up with an excuse to decline the invitation without being rude.

At that precise moment, and to my utter amazement, an almost inexplicable peace came over me as a small still voice within seemed to whisper, *You have all that food you baked, so you can contribute that towards the party.*

I was so surprised by this sudden thought that I immediately accepted the invitation. How was I to know this visit would turn out to be the very reason I felt compelled to bake all that food? I left hurriedly to pick up my children and return with the baking.

The events of the day could not be explained and proved to be more than just a coincidence. The warmth of this experience began to soften my heart and change my concept and attitude towards God. It was not about what I had to do but what Jesus had already done for me. God knew exactly what it would take to get me to understand and accept His grace, mercy, and love.

What an amazing personal, creative God we have, who loves us unconditionally and knows every detail of our lives, including our very thoughts. He has such wonderful things in store for us if we only allow Him to reveal them to us. After the amazing events of that day and filled with hope, I decided to attend the church the following Sunday, accompanied by my children.

I had attended a local church with neighbours a few times when younger, but it was nothing like this. The music was lively. People were happy, and they raised their arms in the air and waved enthusiastically. I thought, *What strange people!* and had a sudden desire to run. To do so, however, would have meant standing up and walking past the congregation to reach the exit at the back of the hall.

Despite tides of fear rising within me, I decided to stay where I was. After a while, I began to lose the sensation of being trapped and started to relax a little. I realised I actually enjoyed the music and the singing. I loved music as a child and remember my mother singing around the house, and how I used to join in. And after the service, I was pleasantly surprised at how friendly all the people were.

I started to go to church regularly and enjoyed it more and more. Listening to the message delivered by the pastor definitely helped relieve the sense of loneliness and despair that often haunted me.

I felt God was beginning to penetrate my heart, and the church was somewhere I could feel safe and accepted. There were no probing or embarrassing questions. It was just like being part of a big family, although very different from the one I had been brought up in. The genuine love shown by the people there was overwhelming, and I truly felt I had found a new home. I spent many precious hours at the home of Pastor Trevor, his wife, Isabel, and their four children.

My Feelings for Today

I want to sing and paint my feelings

in pictures for everyone to see.

I want to read and understand

life's meaningful poetry.

I want to be me as I see myself,

but most of all, I want to say

I need to share this love of life

I feel so strong today.

Today

I feel like I am in love with life, surrounded
by an awareness of beautiful things and feelings
that have been shut off for so long,
I guess because of all the hurt and pain
that life sometimes brings.

Through all the negatives in life
I am sure we often find
that we can share with someone else
our experience and say, hey look
I've been there, let me help you through,
just being there, showing you care
will give them peace of mind.

I have often yearned for happiness,
searched for things I did not have,
yet it is now that I have learned
through my experience in life happiness
must first be found within ourselves.

For life is love, and love of life
is there for us to find,
and we have lived and learned from life
when we can simply say,
the past is gone, future yet to come,
but now is here, and here is now,
live from day to day.

So do not waste your life away,
wishing for things that have not come,
the little things in life are there
for you to take and mould
into something you will always have
to cherish and to hold
in your loving chain
of memories.

The Joy of the Lord

Opening the door of my heart to the possibility of receiving God's love filled me with confidence and a strong desire to drag myself out of the pit of misery and despair in which I had lived for so long. I did not really understand what was happening, but I was very excited about the fact I might at last be able to stand on my own two feet.

It was almost as if I was standing in a dark, long tunnel, still in the midst of pain and confusion. But for the first time in my life, I saw a ray of hope, literally a light at the end of the tunnel and a future that did not depend on my own strength or ability.

I knew without doubt that God had touched me. My heart was so full of His love I thought it would burst. I began to express newfound joy and sad memories in the form of poetry as the Lord began to heal me.

I wanted to write down each tiny step of faith I had taken and how Jesus had changed my life. As my faith and knowledge of God's Word increased, I recorded every aspect of God's life-changing effect on my life. The incredible thing is that I had never written any poetry prior to this. In fact, I was not very good in English at school. So for me to experience this overflow of poetry was quite remarkable. I knew it had to be God's inspiration and guidance. There is no way in the natural that I can write like that.

As I began to trust God and allow Him to touch my heart, I became aware of the fact I had also locked away the pain and frustration from the many deep wounds of the past. I wanted so much to move forward and receive all God's blessings. However, painful experiences, memories, and learned responses held me captive for many years.

God, in His infinite wisdom and intimate knowledge, understood my reluctance and found ways in which to pour His abundant love into my fragile heart. Gradually, He brought to the surface every painful experience from my childhood, showing me how to deal with the rejection and hurt. He understood the affect my painful history was also having on my children and opened the eyes of my understanding to their specific physical, emotional, and spiritual needs.

If God was going to heal us, I was going to have to be totally honest with Him and those I had come to trust. I had to accept the fact I was not solely responsible for everything that had happened in our lives.

I would come to understand that God was a God of love, and forgiveness and the agape love of God were vastly different than the love we experience in the natural. Buckets of tears were shed as God revealed and healed many painful memories, while at the same time, cleansing my heart and mind.

Each step God and I took together left indelible impressions on my heart of how awesome He is. Mercifully, the intense emotional pain began to dwindle and was replaced by a new awareness and a sense of excitement and hope.

The First Step

In the past I can honestly say
I had more than my share of troubles and fears.
Why? was the question I asked time after time;
no answer I found, though
I tried through the years.

Then one day I ran into a friend
who had often been down, like I was then;
as we talked, I became very aware
of the love she had found and wanted to share;
dare I hope that love could be mine.

Those first steps to Jesus, I will never forget;
the love of His people with whom I have met
brings so much hope and feelings of love
the source can only be our Father above.

Many tears have been shed, though not in vain,
Jesus' love I found dissolves all hurt and pain;
thank you, God's children, for His love that you teach
from people like me, whose needs are so great
yet seem so hard to reach.

New Hope in Life

The small steps of faith we take with the Lord are similar to those of a child learning to walk. A child will intently focus on the person encouraging him or her to take that first step alone. The child's confidence is not in his or her own ability but in the faith and trust placed in others. The desire to walk is so strong the child is able to overcome fear, confident that Mum or Dad will catch them if they fall. So it is with our heavenly Father. As we begin to step out in faith, He steps out with us and is there to catch us if any obstacle causes us to stumble.

Like a child, our first step of faith is always the hardest. Although we may fall, sometimes hurting more than our ego, a strength from within and encouragement from others urge us to go on. We believe in what we are doing, and each step forward brings a new level of freedom and courage.

With freedom comes greater opportunity for us to explore and get into all sorts of mischief. There will be falls, bumps, and tears along the way. But all things considered, it is a great time of learning and excitement.

> The steps of a good man are directed by the Lord. He delights in each step they take. If they fall it isn't fatal, for the Lord holds them with His hand. (Psalm 37:23–24)

Prayer

Father God, you alone know the condition of my damaged soul, because You have watched my every step since the time of my birth. Storms in my life have blinded me to the truth of Your mercy and grace. I ask in Jesus' name for Your Spirit to encourage and enlighten my steps as I uncover the golden threads of faith, hope, and love that had been delicately woven into the fabric of my life. Amen.

God's Love

I asked Jesus into my life;
my heart feels happy and light,
that which once seemed empty
now is full and bright.

Nowhere else can we find
security and peace of mind,
precious gifts wrapped in love,
flowing freely from above.

Day by day, He proves how much
He loves and cares for us;
my life I gladly place in His hands,
my love, above all, I give to Jesus.

There is no turning back for me.
He is in my heart I know
through faith in Jesus and His Word
this love I feel will surely grow.

Just like the branches of a tree,
so everyone who is lost will see
the strength, love, peace, and
faith in God has given me.

The Depth of God's Love

God's love is unfathomable and perfect. He expressed that love by allowing His Son, Jesus, to be put to death on the cross over two thousand years ago. Jesus lives to intercede for us, praying we will become more like Him, so the love He shows us we can, in turn, show others. We can do this if we bare our hearts to Him and allow Him to deal with areas of our lives that might hinder us reaching that precious goal.

God's love and primary concern is restoring all humankind to a loving relationship with Him. The gift of His love is offered to all who believe in Him. It is through accepting this love that we are able to minister to others and show them how much God loves and cares for them. To achieve this, we need to surrender anything that might hinder our relationship with God and our trust in Him. As we grow in the knowledge of God and His goodness, we become more able to do this. God sets us free, free from the past and the bitterness and hurt that can so easily stunt our growth. Forgiveness is the key. Oh that we could have the heart attitude of God, who freely forgives all who are truly sorry and want to start again. His loving arms wait to surround all who are prepared to try.

I bless the holy name of God with all my heart.

Yes, I will bless the Lord and not forget the glorious things he does for me. He forgives all my sins. He heals me. (Psalm 103:1–3)

Prayer

Lord, I see Your love flowing freely from the hearts of Your people and become discouraged when I am not able to do that, too. The scars on my heart remind me of the times I trusted and was deeply wounded. Help me to trust You more and let go of the bitterness and anger that has kept me in bondage. Please heal my broken heart, and fill it instead with Your perfect love. Amen.

The Way

A message deep within my heart
I know is meant for all,
for God is waiting patiently
to hear our faintest call.

He gently took me by the hand
said, "Let me help you understand."
Abundant seeds of love to sow,
need rain and sun in which to grow
into something lasting and beautiful.

For when we open up our heart
to Jesus, to our surprise we find
that love just grows and overflows,
like dewdrops settling down
on lonely people everywhere,
so many of them around.

Waiting there for someone
to show to them the way
to God, the Father, through Jesus,
new hope this very day.

Jesus Is the Only Way to God

God in His gentleness and love has faithfully led and encouraged me in ways I thought were not possible. His timing is always perfect. It is Jesus who prepares the way for us. It is sometimes hard to understand how this works, but when we see God working in the lives of others, it increases our faith to believe He can do the same for us. The greatest hindrance to believing this truth is a sense of failure and guilt, which can bring about low self-esteem.

I learned God's willingness to work in our lives has nothing to do with the estimation of our own self-worth. He is like a dedicated gardener, planting seeds of love in our hearts and watering them by the truth of His Word. Warmed by the sun, the seeds grow into beautiful trees in the same way our faith grows, and our hearts and minds are enlightened by His wisdom and love. This understanding helps us to minister to others and show them how He wants to meet all their needs.

When I first asked Jesus to come into my life, the joy that flooded my soul was all consuming. I was desperately keen to tell others about Him but seemed to lack the confidence to do so. This initial fear soon passed, however, and I found myself stepping out in faith and sharing with others. Being able to witness freely about Jesus and what He did in my life released a wellspring of joy in my heart.

Jesus told him, I am the way—yes, and the truth and the life.

No one can get to the Father except by means of me. (John 14:6)

Prayer

Lord, You have revealed a pathway of light and love that fills my heart with joy and hope for a brighter future. Let not my head be bowed in shame any longer, for You have saved me for a purpose, redeemed my life from destruction, and crowned my head with loving kindness. Amen.

God's Beauty

Have you ever watched a sunset
going down before your eyes?
The red and gold mingles
so perfectly it makes you realize
a precious work of God is there,
so peaceful yet so bright
few people really stop to share
the beauty of God's eternal light.

So take the time right now,
my friend, to lift your heavy load.
Leave your worries and your cares
behind you on the road.
The love of God so radiant,
and with the beauty of the world,
sunsets and such are just signs
of a beautiful peace and love
which can be yours and mine
when we give our lives to the Lord.

*As you travel up the path
to Jesus, you will find
so much beauty on the way.
You'll feel you have been blind,
for every step you take you'll see
the beauty God has given thee.
Share with others while you can;
so many of our fellow men are
blind and cannot see.*

Eyes Opened to God's Beauty

Being in love changes our whole outlook on life. It is as though we are wearing rose-coloured spectacles, and we see beauty in everything around us.

Having lived on the west coast of Australia all my life, I have been truly blessed with the most magnificent sunsets. One night while standing on my veranda and watching the sun go down, I beheld a majestic sight as the perfect balance of red-to-crimson and gold-to-orange hues mingled together that seemed to radiate God's awesome presence.

The sky portrayed so much life and light, whilst at the same time producing a level of tranquillity I had not experienced before. My eyes were opened to the beauty of God's love, and I literally felt His presence. At the same time, a new poem began to form in my heart.

Constantly during our Christian walk, we need to think back to the time when we first tasted God's love, and remember how He graciously gave us a new lease on life. We need to always remember how He has provided us with the strength and courage to go on and overcome any doubts and fears that might arise.

> You have patiently suffered for me without quitting, yet there is one thing wrong; you don't love me as at the first. Think about those times of your first love. (Revelation 2:3–4)

Prayer

Lord, Your splendid rays of light and warmth fill our hearts with love and understanding. We stand in Your presence in awe and wonder, and when storm clouds gather in our lives, we are confident You will never leave or forsake us. Amen.

A Loving Spark

Slowly the sun fades in the West,
the earth becomes a silhouette,
water on the lake is still,
upon the hilltops the trees
gently sway in the breeze.

A fire is lit upon the ground,
night is still; we gather 'round,
we talk, we laugh and sing,
flames are dancing in the night,
stars above are shining bright,
we need not worry the Lord is there;
only He knows what tomorrow will bring.

For each of us He has a plan,
being moulded by His loving hand,
He places in our hearts a spark
and gently blows a breeze
to give us warmth and light within,
and sets our troubled minds at ease.

So much beauty for us He shares
just to prove how much He cares;
thank You, Lord, for the spark
You carefully tended in the dark.

A Loving Spark

Spending time with family and friends is truly special. I remember how my church family gathered at barbecues and picnics in the bush near Kalgoorlie. We had lots of fun sitting around the campfire, singing songs and laughing. Life seemed so good in those days. We were young and innocent, totally unaware of the events that were to unfold in our lives.

I remember the flames dancing in the night sky and the fire's sparks rising gently upwards with seemingly not a care in the world. The branches high in the beautiful gum trees swayed slightly, and the leaves rustled as the wind passed through them.

What an awesome setting that was. And how wonderful it is to be able to look at things in the natural and reflect on how they show God's creation. The depth of this revelation draws us into a closer relationship with Him and helps us determine His will and purpose for our lives.

God's provision for nature is apparent even in the harsh Australian bush environment. Despite the almost desert conditions, trees continue to grow, providing shade for birds and animals during the heat of the day. Emus rest in the shadows, and kangaroos sleep under salt bushes, waiting for the cool of the evening before they set out to forage for food.

As each new day dawns, the sun provides light and heat. And when storm clouds appear in the sky, they often herald the arrival of short bursts of torrential rain. When the thunder and lightning ceases, God signals the end of the storm with the appearance of a beautiful rainbow. When we take the time to stop and really listen to the call of the wild, it is not hard to believe in God and to trust Him for all our needs.

> Don't worry about things, food, drink and clothes. For you already have life and a body and they are far more important than what to eat and wear. Look at the birds! They don't worry about what to eat, they don't sow or reap or store up food, for your heavenly Father feeds them. And you are far more valuable to him than they are. Will all your worries add a single moment to your life. (Matthew 6:25–27)

Prayer

Lord, I am constantly amazed at Your loving care and concern for Your beloved creation. Forgive us for doubting your ability to provide all our needs, and teach us to understand the difference between our needs and our wants. Amen.

Castles in the Sand

I built my castle in the sand,
towers around my strength,
labored hard to build the walls,
secure at last this was my land.

I ventured out to seek the Lord
and slowly moved away
from my castle in the sand
a little more each day.

It seemed to me that I had made
a pathway in between,
in which I travelled back and forth,
depending on my need.

The Lord knew I was ready
for another step to take.
He had shown to me His love;
it was time to make the break.
Down came the rain and washed
away my castle in the sand.

I will build again, I know,
according to God's plan,
another castle step by step,
guided by His loving hand.

My Castle Built upon the Sand

During occasional childhood trips to the coast, we used to build sand castles, destroy them, and start all over again. What a contrast there is between the foundation of these castles made of sand, on which many of us build our lives, and the foundation of rock on which we build our lives in Christ.

God's free gift of love was made available to us through His precious Son, Jesus Christ. He is the only foundation secure enough to enable us to withstand the storms that can appear in our lives.

Shortly after inviting Jesus into my heart, I learned I could trust God with more of my life. I felt encouraged and strengthened when I spent time with other believers. Fellowship is very important to Christians, and the best way to achieve this is by attending church. This is particularly important for new believers.

Without regular fellowship, sharing, and encouragement, we can sometimes falter in our walk with the Lord. We can be torn between what we know is right in the sight of God and what our heart desires.

It is so easy to step back into the well-worn footprints in the sand, which are comfortable and seem to be a perfect fit. How soon we forget the dangers of the rising tides and effects of sandstorms that dim our vision. Even though we have become a "new creation" in Christ, we are not immune to temptation. But there is nothing God cannot or will not forgive if we are honest with Him and others we trust to help us overcome. Our perceived guilt and shame often cause us to withdraw.

Not long after I was saved, I took ill and was hospitalised with a severe kidney complaint. I ended up spending over two months in hospital and was forced to rely on family and friends to care for my children. Every aspect of my perceived independence and self-worth was challenged.

I often lay there wondering what God might be trying to show me in this circumstance and where I might have gone wrong. I could not understand what had brought this calamity upon me. At one stage, I honestly thought God had abandoned me and fought temptation to rebuild the protective walls around my heart.

This time in hospital actually proved to a perfect opportunity for God to show me how to rise above fear and distrust. A young woman facing similar health issues and trusted God happened to be in the same ward as I. Once more I learned by the example of others.

> All who listen to my instructions and follow them are wise, like a man who builds his house on solid rock. Though the rain comes in torrents, and the floods rise and the storm winds beat against his house, it won't collapse, for it is built on rock. (Matthew 7:24–25)

Prayer

I thank You, God, that You are a loving Father, who keeps His children on the pathway of righteousness. And when You cause a door to close in our lives, You always open a window of opportunity. Help me to understand that all that happens to us is working for our good if we love You and are fitting into Your plans. Amen.

A Child's Plea

A child stands amongst the crowd,
his arms stretched out wide,
people rushing to and fro.
No one really sees God's child,
he waits and watches, very aware
of the love He feels and wants to share.

Won't someone please look and see
what this lifestyle is doing to me?
How can you expect me to grow up secure
without a foundation for me to endure
the hurt and pain which will come my way
as world problems increase day by day?

He sees the world through innocent eyes,
to him life is simple; it just takes a smile,
touch of a hand, cuddle, or kiss.
Surely that's something grown-ups won't miss,
but a sign that means someone is there
to give, to love, and to show they care.

So let all us grownups practice to be
as a child of God, with vision to see
God's love is the only foundation we need
to change this world in all its greed
back into the beautiful place it was
when the earth was God's creation of love.

A Child's Plea

The deepest wound in my heart resulted from not being able to give my children the security and peace I had longed for in my childhood. My children were loved by both families, but I felt bad I was not able to protect them from the confusion and heartache that went with a traumatic separation and subsequent divorce.

We learn our relationship skills from our parents, and it is very sad when one parent dominates the other. When any form of abuse is present, unhealthy relational patterns are set in motion. We cannot give our children what we do not have ourselves. It is important to understand how this pattern of controlling behaviour and abuse works and take corrective action to prevent it from continuing through our children.

We need to acknowledge any signs of domination and abuse in our lives and take the necessary steps to free ourselves from the bondage of destructive relationships. To do this we have to first change the way we think, and we need to ask the Lord for help in doing this. A change of heart and attitude is necessary, or we risk remaining in the circumstances we feel trapped in.

God's Word is the light that shines in the darkness and reveals a new and better way to live in peace and harmony. Each courageous step towards knowledge and understanding in these areas breaks a link in the generational chain of abuse and helplessness.

The voice of fear that has kept us in bondage for so long will rise and demand our attention. But He who calls us out of fear is faithful and will not let us fail.

Blessed are the peace makers, for they shall be called the children of God. (Matthew 5:9)

Prayer

Lord, help us to fully understand the precious gift of free will You bestowed on humankind. This gift to choose whom we love, serve, and obey comes with many blessings and much responsibility. Grant us wisdom and compassion to lovingly teach and support all those who are oppressed and feel helpless in their circumstance. Amen.

Memories

Stop a moment; do you recall
some warm, precious moments gone by
to stand with a friend in the night,
sharing a vision up in the sky,
a blanket of beautiful starlight?

Warmth and peace for you and your friend,
time moves on, and you don't understand
why this beautiful night must come to an end.

Memories like these are ours to hold
when the days darken and nights grow cold;
in amongst our troubles, a warmth begins to glow,
recalling these special moments we know,
giving us hope and strength to go on
in search of the happiness we knew and has gone.

Memories

When the power inside our house went off unexpectedly, we were thrown into darkness. We had to feel our way through the house to get to the back door. Once outside, there was always sufficient light from the moon and stars to be able to make our way safely around obstacles.

Spending countless hot summer nights sleeping out under the stars as a child, opened my eyes to God's creative ability and beauty. The outback night sky is always crystal clear, with millions of stars sparkling like diamonds against a background of black velvet. It is not hard to see the awesomeness of God and His creation. We have become so dependent on our ability to meet our own needs and often forget these things are temporal, unlike the things God created and provided for us.

He is the Creator of light and purposely made two great lights—the greater light (the sun) to rule the day and the lesser light (the moon) to rule the night. He also made the stars, the uncountable millions of them. When we stumble and fall into spiritual darkness, God is ever there to shine His glorious light on us and illuminate the correct pathway to take. We have only to look beyond our reasoning and believe.

> He counts the stars and calls them by name. How great He is! His power is absolute! His understanding is unlimited. He covers the heavens with clouds, sends down showers and makes grass grow in mountain pastures. But His joy is in those who reverence Him,

those who expect him to be loving and kind. (Psalm 147:4, 5, 8, 11)

Prayer

Father God, we are but tiny specks in the universe compared to the magnificence of one star in the heavens, which You have created and called by name. Help us to understand that we are far more valuable to You than even the brightest star, and Your joy comes from personal relationship with each and every one of us. Amen.

Sharing with Friends

Everyone needs friends who care
when life seems neither here nor there;
God never intended us to be alone
or to carry a heavy load on our own,
but to share with our friends
both the good times and bad,
heartache and happiness we have all had.

A friendship built in this kind of way
is one that lasts through any long day.
One important thing we must all learn,
a lasting friendship is one we must earn.
If you have such a friendship, value its worth;
don't trade it for any treasures of earth.

There will come a time when you must part,
and you will feel a loss deep in your heart;
time and distance is just a small test.
Your friendship won't change,
you both did your best.

Though you will grow and take different paths,
the joy of knowing your friendship will last
makes all the sharing, taking, and giving
life worth the effort, life worth living.

Sharing with Friends

It is important to have close friends with whom we can share our feelings and emotions. We make many friends during our lives, and from time to time, meet a special one who becomes our "best" friend. This is particularly true during our childhood years. True friends are the ones with whom we can share our innermost secrets and who are genuinely interested in helping us overcome difficult situations in our lives. When we can confide, laugh, and cry with them, their friendship can be so precious that they become as gemstones.

There comes a time we lose friends when they move away. The amazing thing is that although we may not see them for several years, when we do meet up again, the relationship is the same. It is as if time has stood still.

When I think of precious friends and the memories we share, a joy fills my heart. Yet even though I love my friends dearly, I know that no human friendship will ever equal the intimate friendship I have with Jesus. He is the one referred to in the Scriptures as the "friend who sticks closer than a brother" (Proverbs 8:24).

> But for you O Israel, you are mine, my chosen ones. For you are Abrahams family and he was my friend. Fear not for I am with you, be not dismayed, I am your God. I will strengthen you, I will help you...
>
> I will uphold you with my victorious right hand" (Isaiah 41:8, 10)

Prayer

Lord Jesus, I thank You for the many beautiful friends You have placed in my life over the years, and who have faithfully walked with me in fair and foul weather. Their examples of forgiveness, patience, and compassion have paved the way to a deeper understanding of Your commitment, and love towards our eternal friendship. Amen.

Peace

While looking for tomorrow
I somehow missed today,
the peace I longed so much for
had been lost along the way.

I was portrayed as a ship
carried out to sea,
unable to control the waves
which were playing chess with me.

I called the Lord; He rescued me,
wind died down, He calmed the sea.
I saw a light that would never dim,
a ray of peace, I felt within.

Now I am sailing with the Lord,
being led according to His Word
my life has been so much changed
I feel content
the Lord rearranged my life
so I would find His peace.
The peace, love and hope
there for us all, if we but seek
the Lord and dare to call.

Peace and Harmony with God

Adam and Eve lived in a perfect environment, where God provided for their every need, be it physical, emotional, or spiritual. They were given the precious gift of free will—the ability to choose whom to love, serve, and obey, as indeed we have today. Their deliberate act of disobedience by eating the fruit of the forbidden tree separated them from God and His blessings.

God is a God of righteousness, which simply means to be in "right standing" with Him. Even if we sin by accident or design, we have access to God through Jesus Christ and can seek His forgiveness. The Bible tells us God is "faithful and just to forgive our sins and to cleanse us from all unrighteousness" (1 John 1:9).

The Lord encourages us in His Word to pray to Him if we are anxious about anything, and He desires to restore us to fellowship with Him if we admit our shortcomings. God knows us intimately and is loving and forgiving. He is like a loving parent who desires to guide and teach us.

As loving parents, we teach our children not to touch a hot stove, because we know the consequence if they do so. By this they learn obedience, so when temptation comes, they will remember what they have been told. If we do this in love, there is a far better chance they will obey our instructions than be naughty, ignoring us and getting hurt.

We all have a conscience, even at a young age. A child knows inherently the difference between right and wrong. Disobedience can cloud our perception and dim the light of truth. The result of our disobedient actions can leave us feeling fearful and wanting to hide our heads in shame. I often wonder how different things may have been for humankind if Adam and Eve had been honest with God when He called to them in the garden of Eden after they disobeyed his instructions.

For a time I was led by my own desires. That placed me at the helm of my destiny and lifeboat. With no clear direction, my small vessel was tossed on the tide of indecision until I no longer felt safe. I called out to the Lord, and despite my disobedience to His loving instructions, He heard my faint cry over the winds of adversity and set out to rescue me.

The most important lessons in life are often learned from making mistakes and having to live with the consequences. If we humble ourselves before Him and seek His guidance, we are less likely to make many of the common mistakes in life and to live a life of peace and harmony with God.

> Don't worry about anything: instead pray about everything: tell God your needs and don't forget to thank him for his answers. If you do this you will experience God's peace, which is far more wonderful than the human mind can understand. His peace will keep your thoughts and hearts quiet and at rest as you trust in Christ Jesus" (Philippians 4:6–7)

Prayer

Lord, your faithfulness never ceases to amaze me. I am humbled by Your willingness to always lead me back to the truth and the light of your abundant love and care. Amen.

Take a Step

If you are feeling lonely
or you think that no one cares,
just lift your thoughts to Jesus
and come to Him in prayer,
take a step and walk in faith,
for the Lord is always there.

A Lord that never goes away,
He is faithful through and through.
just tell Jesus how you feel,
and believe He will comfort you.

Then open up your heart in praise
to our heavenly Father above;
thank Him for His faithfulness,
then you will find your
saddened thoughts have gone,
replaced with thoughts of love.

God Is Faithful

It is one thing to read about the promises of God in the Bible and another to truly believe them in our hearts. It is difficult, especially if we feel unworthy to receive His love and mercy.

In an earlier chapter, I spoke of the importance of being honest with God and with people we know we can trust. Ours is an all-powerful, ever-present, and all-knowing God, so we cannot hide from Him. He even knows the number of hairs on our head. Knowing this and the depth of His love, it is not hard to understand why His desire is for us to believe in and trust Him. His blessings are new every morning. And great is His faithfulness, which is acknowledged numerous times in hymns and songs of praise.

We have to understand that God loves and accepts us as we are. The key we hold in our hand, which opens the floodgates of His abundant blessings, is simply faith, believing He is who He says He is. The love of God is a gift. There is nothing we can do to earn that love, "Because of his kindness you have been saved through trusting Christ. And even trusting is not of yourselves; It too is a gift from God" (Ephesians 2:8).

While sitting in my car one sunny afternoon, waiting to collect my son from kindergarten, a peace filled my heart, and I sensed a poem rising in my spirit. I had nothing to write on except an empty cigarette packet someone had left in my car. As I started to scribble the words, I realised it was a poem about loneliness. This seemed strange, as I was not actually feeling lonely at that particular time.

Four days later, I realised the purpose for that particular verse. I faced a situation in which I felt totally alone and unloved. As children, the only joy in our lives was the special little birthday parties our mother put on for us. This year, for no apparent reason, everyone I knew forgot my birthday. By four o'clock that afternoon, doubt and depression began to set in.

My birthday had always been something I looked forward to, and I was devastated no one in my family or church remembered. As I lay on my bed, it dawned on me that God in His infinite love and wisdom had forewarned me and wanted to teach me how to trust Him and praise Him regardless of circumstances. What a loving heavenly Father we have! Not only does He see each step on the pathway of our lives, He gives us an extra portion of His love and strength that we might be able to face each new crisis with confidence. With the correct heart attitude we are far more able to cope with adversity when it strikes.

> Moreover, because of what Christ has done, we have become gifts to God that He delights in. For as part of God's sovereign plan we were chosen from the beginning to be His and all things happened just as He decided long ago. God's purpose in this was that we should praise God and give glory to Him for doing these mighty things for us, who were the first to trust in Christ. (Ephesians 1:11–12)

Prayer

Lord, You know the beginning and the end of my days and delight in each step of faith I take. Thank You for the seeds of love You plant in our hearts so we can pick fresh flowers in times of sadness. Amen.

Tears of Love

The tears I feel inside today,
I am happy to be able to say,
are overflowing tears of love
for our heavenly Father above.

There is, I find, no earthly way
to start our lives anew,
forget the past, and find His love
so pure, strong, and true.

Oh Lord! How can I express
this love I feel so strong,
how wonderful it is to be blessed
and know to whom our hearts belong?

Having a Thankful Heart

Have you ever experienced a depth of emotion so powerful that it made you want to cry?

I often reflect on the many ways in which God has revealed Himself to me during my journey through life with Him. I am always overwhelmed by a sense of love and gratitude. He is a good God, who can heal bitter memories and feelings of inadequacy. His love is like a river flowing from the depths of my heart, and it is difficult to control the tears that flow down my cheeks when I think of everything He has done for me. Considering the destructive relationship I had with my father. It is a miracle that God has been able to reveal His Father heart to me.

God's love for humankind is so great that He willingly gave His only beloved Son that we might all experience abundant life here on earth and become heirs to His grace and mercy. In return, He asks us to give our lives back to him. And as we do so by an act of our will, He frees us from guilt and confusion, restoring us to health and prosperity. When we understand the magnitude of the price He paid for us by dying on the cross, how can we possibly deny Him our time and talent in helping bring others to the knowledge of Him? No wonder the Scriptures tell us, "Greater love has no one than this, that he lay down his life for his friends" (John 15:3).

> And so dear brothers, I plead with you to give your
> bodies to God, let them be a living sacrifice, holy—the
> kind He can accept. When you think of what He has

63

done for you, is this too much to ask? Don't copy the behaviour and customs of this world, but be a new and different person with a fresh awareness in all that you do and think. Then you will learn from your own experience how His ways will really satisfy you. (Romans 12:1)

Prayer

Lord, You have loved me unconditionally and forgiven my many mistakes as we walked together on the path of personal discovery and inner healing. Help me to be more like Your precious Son, Jesus, in thought, word, and deed. Amen.

Praise God

A child of God you have become,
give praise, for you and He are one,
above all creation on this earth,
He chose you and saw within your worth.

Then in a special loving way,
strengthened you day by day,
allowed tests and trials for you to face,
thus helping you to grow in grace,
carefully moulding and working deep within,
only Jesus knew what peace it would bring.

Now you know the peace and love,
joy and guidance from above,
overflowing love for others
warms the heart of your brothers,

Starlight flickering in the night,
truth revealed as rays of light,
seeds of love are grown in faith,
glory to Jesus for keeping them safe
until He placed you on their ground,
so you could share what you have found.

A beautiful way to start life over again,
experience light where darkness has been;
through Jesus Christ our sins are forgiven,
His footsteps reveal the pathway to heaven.

Sharing God's Love

When Adam and Eve were banished from the presence of their beloved Creator and Father God, the eyes of their understanding were opened to the choices of good and evil set before them. Their sons, Cain and Abel, did not have the intimacy their parents shared with God in the garden of Eden. So their instruction in righteousness was second hand, so to speak. Rules without a personal, loving relationship are often misunderstood and hard to accept. Abel chose to learn from his parents' mistakes, whereas Cain developed a selfish attitude and went against their advice. Unresolved resentment and jealousy caused him to murder his only brother.

All through the Old Testament, there are examples of how God raised up people who, despite the personal cost involved, chose to follow Him and learn His ways. They were given mandates to reveal God's desire to be reunited with His entire beloved creation.

In the wilderness, God's presence guided the Israelites by a cloud during the day and a pillar of fire by night. He provided protection for them as He guided them towards the land of promise, performing many miracles to show His faithfulness.

Future generations did not trust God, especially one they could not see. They needed a living example to reveal by word and deed how much God still loved them. To do this, He sent His only begotten Son into the world as a babe to grow up experiencing the love, joy, hardship, pain, rejection, and sorrow we continue to experience today.

Jesus knew the personal sacrifice and suffering He would have to endure to accomplish the will of his Father and reunite us with Him.

He chose by an act of His will to leave his kingdom in heaven and temporarily put aside His glory to testify of His Father and provide a way for humankind to be redeemed and obtain eternal life.

> For from the beginning God decided that those who came to Him, and all along He knew who would— should become like his Son, so that his Son would be the first, with many brothers. (Romans 8:29)

Prayer

Father God, having received this precious gift of eternal life from You, how can I not allow Your rays of light and the warm heart of Your Son to touch the lives of others? Give me the courage I need to witness in Your name. Amen.

To Walk with God's Spirit

To walk with God's Spirit
allows His Spirit within
to change the direction
of where we have been,
opening our eyes
to the Word of the Lord
by the grace gift of God
to those He has called.

To walk in the Spirit
and let it be seen
a great beam of light
where darkness has been,
a new song to sing
and new prayer to pray,
bringing glory to Jesus
each step of the way.

The Spirit of God Leads Us into All Truth

The first twelve months of my Christian walk meant learning to love, trust, and obey the simple instructions of God. Every character flaw revealed became a new challenge and stepping stone across the river of confusion in my life. As I took each small step of faith, God revealed His faithfulness, and I was encouraged to seek more understanding of Him and His purpose for my life.

Having been saved by His mercy, love, and grace, I had a strong desire to be water baptized, just as Jesus had been in the River Jordan. This would take place during a church camp in the coastal town of Esperance in Western Australia, in the Southern Ocean. This ocean is fed by currents of freezing cold water from Antarctica, many thousands of kilometres to the south.

The wintery conditions of the day could not dampen my enthusiasm. As we stood shivering, waiting for the rain to stop, I was reminded of a song we sang in church called, "Walking, Leaping, and Praising God." On entering the water, each icy wave caused me to leap a little, and I heard the words of the song ringing in my ears. Approaching the site chosen for my baptism, excitement and warmth surrounded my heart.

God's timing is always perfect, and exactly one year to the day from the time I had cried out to God, my water baptism signified a very personal cleansing and change of direction in my life. It was time to turn the page, close that chapter of my life, and begin a new one.

The fine, golden threads of faith, hope, and love God carefully wove into the tapestry of my life from the beginning were finally uncovered. And although there is still evidence of the stains on the fabric of my heart, they serve only as a reminder of the faithfulness and loving concern of my heavenly Father.

> After His baptism, the Holy Spirit descended upon Him in the form of a dove and a voice from Heaven said "This is my beloved Son, and I am wonderfully pleased with Him." (Matthew 4:16–17)

Prayer

Father God, I thank You for weaving golden threads of faith, hope, and love into the tapestry of our lives. Red dust storms and muddy waters may stain beyond recognition, but You, oh Lord, have delivered us from the treacherous waters and set our feet on solid ground. You know the hearts and minds of Your children, and Your faithfulness is unto all generations. Amen.

Epilogue

A hardened heart, high protective walls, and faulty styles of relating did not make it easy for anyone to get close to me. Yet the Father heart of God was touched by the fragility of my wounded heart. Incredible suffering, fear, and lack of understanding of God's love held me captive for twenty-six years. As much as He desired with all His heart to reach out and help me, He could not until I asked Him. He is bound by His Word, and the most precious gift He gives us is free will, giving us the ability to choose whom we love, trust, and obey.

It was not hard for me to relate to Jesus as my brother, Lord, and Saviour, as my older brother was always gentle, loving, and kind. The still small voice of God's precious Holy Spirit had faithfully led me through a maze of confusion during the first twelve months of my Christian walk. However, because of the destructive relationship with my own father, my greatest challenge has been accepting the love and grace of Father God.

My life story is not unlike that of millions of others. Although I do not fully understand why God had me record these tiny steps of faith, I do believe it is His perfect timing to release them. In concluding this chapter of my life, I am very aware of God's call to go deeper and understand more of His heart for His beloved children.

The following personal prayer reveals the true heart of God and His faithfulness to all. May you also be inspired and allow Him to move in your heart. Trust Him with every aspect of your life.

My Personal Prayer

Lord, You reached out and touched me
when I was lost and in despair,
wrapped Your arms around me
and showed You really cared.

Lord, You walked along beside me
as I travelled down each road,
understood each step I took
and shared my heavy load.

Lord, You have shown to me thy wonders,
revealed the meaning of true love,
given me thy word as truth,
and thy Spirit as a dove.

Lord, I know not how much time I have,
and so, I pray to thee
that You will make my ears to hear,
touch my eyes that I may see.

So I will read and know Your Word
and come to fully understand
the way that we have travelled,
run the race that You have planned.

About the Author

Vicki Alicia lives in Mandurah, a coastal town near Perth, Western Australia. She was born and raised in Kalgoorlie-Boulder, which are twin, gold-mining towns east of Perth. The Golden Mile, which was once a chain of individual gold mines stretching across the two towns, later became known as the "Super Pit," the largest, open-pit gold mine in the country.

Her childhood was plagued by loneliness, fear, and rejection which hindered but did not deter her ambition to become a nurse. Rebellion and resentment within her became her sources of strength and determination.

After training as a nurse, Vicki married at the age of seventeen. It seemed to her that all her hopes and dreams had come true, but it did not take her long to realize that "All that glitters is not necessarily gold."

Insecurity, personal loss, grief, and a sense of hopelessness eventually proved to be too much for her, and the marriage failed.

As hard as she tried, she was unable to provide her two children with the love and security lacking in her own childhood.

Vicki spent many years haunted by painful memories from the past. But a chance encounter with someone who spoke to her about God resulted in a sudden and dramatic life change.

The driving force behind this book is a collection of poems written by the author shortly after her encounter with God. These poems portray her feelings and emotions during the early years of her Christian walk.

Her personal journey of faith across a river of hopelessness and despair is a beacon to all who may be searching for truth and purpose in their lives.